I0119557

Josiah C. Long, G. H Brinton

Money inSquabs

Josiah C. Long, G. H Brinton

Money inSquabs

ISBN/EAN: 9783744740234

Printed in Europe, USA, Canada, Australia, Japan

Cover: Foto ©Suzi / pixelio.de

More available books at **www.hansebooks.com**

Money in... Squabs

BY

J. C. LONG and G. H. BRINTON.

PROFUSELY ILLUSTRATED.

WASHINGTON, D. C.,

GEORGE E. HOWARD & CO.,

PUBLISHERS.

COPYRIGHTED AND PRINTED

BY

GEORGE E. HOWARD & CO.

Washington, D. C.

CONTENTS.

PART I - J. C. LONG.

PART II. G. H. BRINTON.

LIST OF ILLUSTRATIONS.

NATIONAL MESSAGE HOLDER FOR HOMING PIGEONS.

Part I.

INTRODUCTORY.

THE gastronomic qualities of the young of the genus *Columba* have long been known and recognized, but their scarcity and consequent high price have always prevented their being plentiful, and a common article of food. Of late years attention has been directed to raising them in large quantities, but the lack of knowledge as to how to proceed has deterred many from attempting the experiment, and turning their attention in this direction. It is for the purpose of aiding and enlightening such novices that this work has been prepared.

As an adjunct to the raising of poultry, small fruits, market gardening and general farming, this industry offers great inducements, as the percentage of profit for the amount of capital invested is large, depending, of course, much on the amount of attention given to it, and the adaptability for the work of the one having it in charge. Hundreds have attempted it and met with disappointment, simply from the fact that they had nothing to guide and encourage them in the way of written experience. It should be commenced by the inexperienced in a small way until thoroughly understood, when they can branch out to an almost unlimited extent. But one should understand before beginning, that it is a business that needs constant attention, and not one that will take care of itself. The breeder and his birds must know each other, and, as far as such a thing is possible, be in perfect harmony.

He must watch his matings to see if they agree, and are both attentive to their duties, to see if they are prolific, good feeders and nurses, and true to one another. If there is a lack of attention to one another and a seeming preference for other mates, such pairs should be separated and remated with those of their choice. If certain pairs prove to be bad feeders and nurses, they should be discarded and replaced by others; for it is all important that your stock should be made up of careful and attentive feeders, as it is only from such parents that you can expect quick growth and maturity, a feature most desirable in commercial squab raising.

It will take time to regulate and establish a satisfactory breeding stud, but in this time you are learning the principles necessary to success and which will eventually enable you to come out a winner. Do not let first disappointments discourage you, but keep persistently at it, studying your birds, and learning lessons from your failures. I would advise beginning with ten or twelve pairs and practicing with them until you understand the work and then increase your numbers gradually. In this way you do not overburden yourself with care, and gradually grow into the business. Commencing in this small way you can easily give it up if you find the work distasteful to you, and, on the other hand, if agreeable it is easy to increase your stock and enlarge your accommodations.

Too many court failure by branching out too extensively at first, before they have had any experience and have learned what it is necessary to know to be successful. The hints contained in this book are such as have been suggested by long experience in this line of work, and any one carefully following them will be at least fairly successful in breeding squabs for market or private use.

The numerous illustrations which have been introduced in this edition will be invaluable to the novice and of much assistance even to the experienced breeder. It has been the aim in preparing this manual to make it a complete illustrated guide and it is believed that none who study the various chapters with care can fail to achieve success in practical pigeon culture.

J. C. LONG.

BREEDING HOUSES.

IN making preparations for squab raising, the first and one of the most important consider-ations is the location of the breeding establish-ment. This should be so situated as to be warm in Winter and not excessively hot in Summer, and above all things where it will be free from damp-ness. For this reason a southern exposure is the best, and if sheltered from the north and west winds, which are those most to be dreaded in the Winter, so much the better.

An expensive structure is not a necessity, although if an entire new building is constructed a certain amount of attention should be given to neatness of appearance, a feature that will not be regretted when finished and ready for occupancy.

Many may not want to go to the expense of erecting a building purposely for breeding, and having barn room may prefer to partition off a portion for the purpose. This can readily be done, although if on an upper floor, entails a greater amount of work in caring for the birds than if nearer the ground. If the upper floor of a barn be used, an aviary or flight should be constructed, as shown in Fig. 1. This flight is essential for keeping the birds healthy and giving them outdoor exercise and fresh air. Such a flight is inexpensive to build, being made of a light framework and covered with one-inch

FIG. 1.

mesh wire. Fig. 2, shows an excellent plan for constructing an aviary on the roof of a house, when
pigeons are kept in an upper or garret room. If the
ground floor be used the southern exposure should be
selected, the apartment well provided with light, and
made, as far as possible, rat and mice-proof. This can
be done by making all joints tight, by tinning around
the lower portion of the partitions and either making
a concrete floor or filling in between the joists on
which the floor is laid, with gravel, slag, or cinders.
Rats cannot work in such material and keep away.
Partitions should be made either of tongued and
grooved boards well seasoned, or twelve-inch boards
well battened and seasoned. This prevents draughts
and aids in keeping the room warm in Winter, a condition much to be desired if squabs are to be raised at

that season, which is the time when they are dearest and consequently bring the best prices. If it is necessary to erect a building let the sills be laid near the ground on

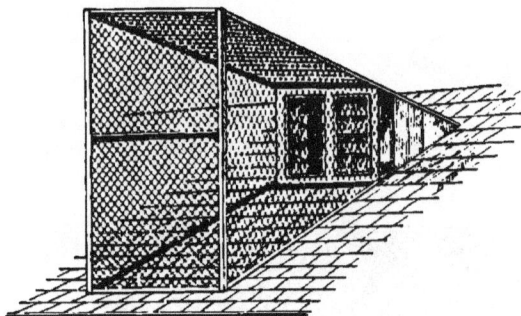

FIG. 2.

flat stones and then fill in between the sleepers, as I have before described, either with cinders, slag, or gravel. If not possible to procure these, then raise it about a foot from the ground, on posts or stone piers, which will allow of space for a cat to move around in and keep the rats away. By boarding up on the sides in Winter and banking with sawdust or turf, leaving a small opening at one end for the cat, it will be warm and dry. For such a building use hemlock or spruce joist, and good seasoned pine lumber tongued and grooved, or with straight edges so that it can be battened. Boards should be sixteen feet long and one inch thick, and if attention is to be paid to neatness dressed on the outside at least. Joist should be of two by four stuff, sixteen feet long. By cutting these in two, making one length eight and a half feet for the front, and the other seven and a half feet for the back, there will be no waste, and it will give the roof all the pitch necessary to shed water well.

The roof can be made of ordinary roofing boards and covered with three-ply tarred roofing paper or felt, which, although it costs a little more at first, is the most economical in the end. If this is then given a good coating of roofing paint, or cement, it will last for years. If shingles are to be had at a low price there can be no better roof if well laid. To secure a house cool in Summer and warm in Winter, it should be ceiled or plastered inside, but as this entails more expense than most people like to incur at first, if the building is lined on the north and west sides with two-ply felt roofing paper it will add to its warmth. If it is also used overhead, it will be an advantage, adding to the warmth in Winter and making it cooler in Summer.

The floor should be made of tongued and grooved flooring, of such a quality as builder can afford. The front should be provided with large windows about six feet apart, and in size about three by six feet. This will give plenty of light, and sunlight in the Winter when the birds are confined to the house by snow and cold weather. Windows should be made so as to slide to the side, that they may be opened and

FIG. 3.

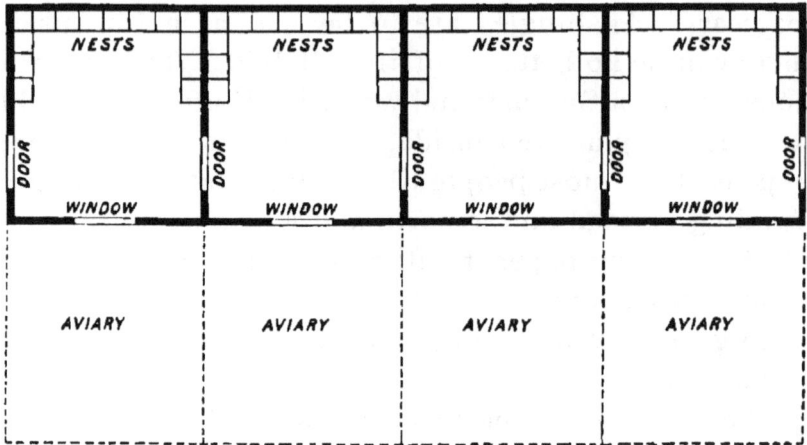

FIG. 4.

closed as necessity requires. Size of lights about seven by nine, and if covered with wire netting there is less liability of breakage.

Ideas vary as to size of house, but one fourteen by sixteen feet floor surface, as shown in Fig. 3, with the heights as before mentioned front and back will accommodate about fifty pairs comfortably. As necessity requires this can be added to indefinitely. But rooms accommodating 100 birds, with communication between each room, I believe to be better than one long room, say to accommodate 1000 birds, as with so many in one room there is bound to be discord. Fig. 4, shows ground plan of a house suitable for 400 birds. This house is fifty-six feet long and sixteen feet wide and is divided into four separate rooms, each being fourteen by sixteen feet in size. It is really four houses joined together like the one shown in Fig. 3. The plan shows arrangement of interior, and location of nests. Fig. 5, is perspective view of the plan.

If it is desired to commence with a few, a house to suit

FIG. 5.

the convenience can be erected. In constructing a house for commercial purposes the door should be made wide enough to admit a wheelbarrow, as there are many times when it will be an advantage to use one inside of the building. Attached to the house on the south side, should be an area or space for the birds to fly in, and have exercise in the open air. This can be made as large as capital will allow and the height of the building, eight and one-half feet. It should be surrounded and covered with wire netting of one-inch mesh, as it prevents the ingress of rats and sparrows, both of which devour the grain, and are in every way objectionable.

The framework can be made of any light material supported on chestnut or cedar posts. Around the run about six feet from the ground should be placed six-inch fence boards, with an occasional one running across from side to side. These are for resting-places for the birds when not on the wing, and will be found to be preferred by them to resting on the ground except when scratching for food or gravel.

The openings for birds to gain access to the area or yard should be about six inches wide and six feet long about four feet from the floor. The door or shutter to these should be hung on hinges on the lower edge, and made to open outwards, on to brackets properly arranged so that when open this door can answer as an alighting-board when birds desire to enter the house. Cords can be so arranged as to close this door at night and at other times when necessary, without entering the building, as in all flocks there are some birds so timid that they fly to the yard as soon as any one enters the apartment.

Besides this main opening one or two smaller open-

GROUP OF HOMERS.

ings can be made six feet from the ground, four inches wide by five inches high, and these arranged with what are known as bolting wires, which are wires so arranged as to swing inwards, and permit any belated bird to enter, and yet when once inside prevent its getting out again. They should be supplied with a small shelf or alighting-board on the outside. The main exits need also an alighting-board or shelf on the inside about five to six inches wide, which can be stationary.

To prevent rats, mice, and other vermin from entering the house through these openings, tin or sheet-iron should be tacked to the building, covering a space two feet below, one foot above, and one foot on either side of the openings. This prevents their getting a foothold, and while they might readily climb up the boards or battens, when they strike the smooth surface of the tin they ease their hold and fall to the ground.

Along the front of the house and about one foot below the roof, on the eight and one-half foot side, cut openings one foot square and eight feet apart, with a key-hole or compass saw. Tack on the top of the pieces of board that come from these openings, strips of leather, replace the pieces and fasten the strip of leather to the remaining portion of the board. Cover the opening on the outside with wire netting to prevent the birds from flying through. Arrange this with cords to raise or lower at will, and you have a small hanging door that can be used as a ventilator on hot days and nights, or at any time when necessary. Should it be thought best to have it closed through cold weather a button placed at the bottom will hold it firmly in place.

Such a house as I have described can be neatly

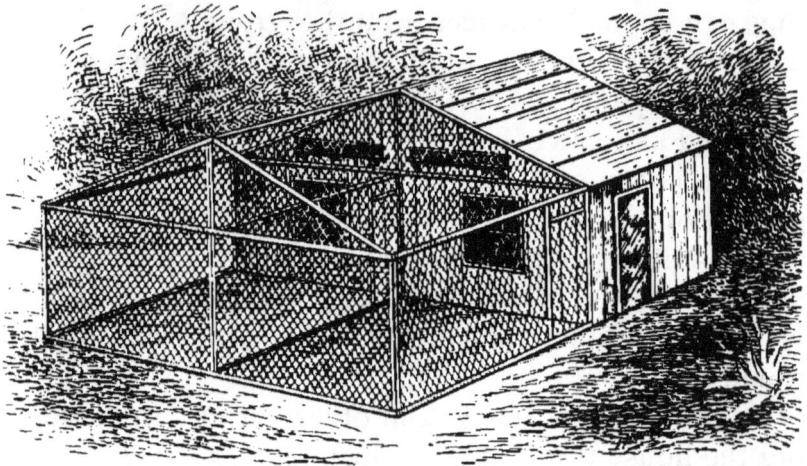

FIG. 6.

painted, whitewashed, or covered with tar cement, which, although not very ornamental, is warm and certainly water-proof. All doors should have spring attachments to them so that they will close of their own accord when any one passes through and thus prevent the birds flying out.

A good plan for a double house is shown in Fig. 6. This house may be built any size desired, according to the number of birds to be kept, but it is not advisable to have the rooms larger than fourteen by sixteen feet each. This house has the double-pitched roof, which may be covered with shingles or tarred paper as may be preferred. Such a house will be found very cheerful and roomy for the birds to breed in, besides presenting a very ornamental appearance.

There are many persons living in cities and suburban places, with back yards as the only places where a pigeon-house could be built. Such persons can, with small expense, keep pigeons for pleasure and profit. In Fig. 7, is shown an excellent plan for a

house in the back yard. The size of the house and
aviary will, of course, depend on the size of the yard
and the inclinations of the builder. The house should
be built snug and tight, rat-proof, and in the farthest
end of the yard.

Having prepared the outside, a few hints as to inside
arrangements will be in order. In each house there
should be a space partitioned off at the entrance, large
enough to hold a few barrels for feed and such imple-
ments as may be needed in cleaning, and when the
building is enlarged to accommodate more birds, this
store-room can be increased according to requirements.

The nests or breeding-boxes, as shown in Fig. 8,
should be made by erecting boards fourteen inches
wide and reaching to the roof on the side opposite the
windows, and about seven feet high on the ends of the
room. Between these upright pieces should be placed
one-inch boards fourteen inches wide, of such length as

FIG. 7.

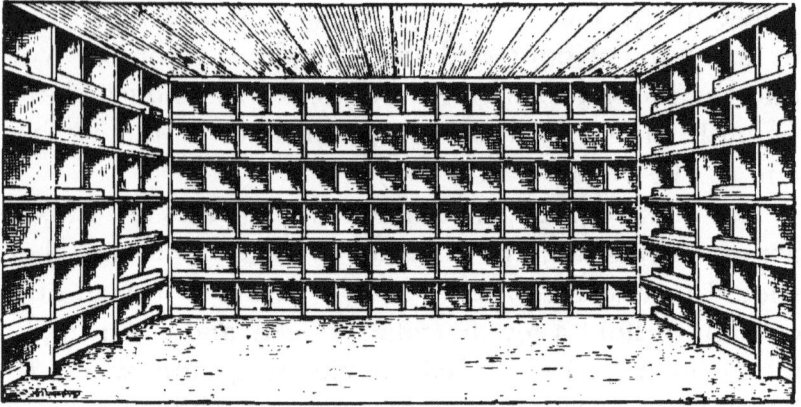

FIG. 8.

space will admit (after taking out the feed-room) twelve inches apart. This will give a series of six shelves. These shelves should be divided into spaces by partitions of fourteen-inch boards, placed twenty inches apart from center to center. This will make a little room or box fourteen by nineteen and one-half by twelve inches. This should be again subdivided by partitions twelve inches high and nine inches wide,

FIG. 9.

thus dividing the larger room into two smaller spaces. In front of these spaces place a strip four inches wide, so arranged as to be easily removed, and there is a breeding-room with two nests, and a walking-board about five inches wide. Fig. 9. shows the nest completed. With such an arrangement each pair of birds has an apartment to itself with two nest-boxes so that, as is frequently the case, if the hen desires to make another nest before the first pair of young are ready to be taken away, she can go into the second apartment and lay and sit undisturbed.

By making nests in this way the pairs are prevented from quarreling, and interfering with one another, and by making the narrow strip in front of the nests movable, they can be easily cleaned. Unless it is necessary to utilize every foot of space the opening under the lower shelf need not be partitioned off. By having a wire framework made to fit the front of each space you can confine a pair of birds to its own apartment if necessary to do so, until they are wonted and settle down satisfied. By a proper arrangement of cleats, all these shelves and partitions can be made movable, so as to be taken down entirely without drawing a nail, when the general times for a thorough cleaning come around. Such a building as here described can be

FIG. 10.

continued to any length desired, but my experience teaches me that it is best to keep the breeding stock in colonies of about one hundred instead of one long building accommodating five or six hundred.

These hints as to construction can be varied and applied by the breeder according to convenience of location and to suit his circumstances and requirements.

Perches should be scattered around the house in all available places for the birds to alight upon. These perches may be built in various ways, according to the individual taste, as shown in Figs. 10 and 11. After the interior is satisfactorily fitted up, and before the breeding stock is admitted, if given a thorough coat of whitewash with a tinge of blue in it, the appearance will be much improved. When persons desire to keep a few pigeons to raise squabs for family use, the same rules will apply as for constructing apartments for commercial purposes.

In many localities where it is desirable to raise squabs in Winter, the breeding room must be artificially heated. This can be done by stoves, or with a regular system of steam heating. The temperature needs to be kept just so that water will not freeze, and that the young will not get chilled when left uncovered by the old birds. If the room is kept too warm it

FIG. 11.

will enervate the breeding birds, be likely to cause them to cast their feathers, and cause results entirely contrary to what is desired. Unlike fancy pigeons, squabs raisers want to be induced to bring out as many as possible during the Winter months, as this is the time for best prices, and whatever course is best to bring about such results is the one to adopt.

BREEDING STOCK.

WITH the breeding-house satisfactorily constructed and arranged, the next move to make is to properly stock it for breeding, and this is one of the most important factors in breeding squabs for market, and one that it will take some time to bring about.

To throw a promiscuous lot of birds together, without regard to variety or color, is not the thing. While they may all be mated pairs, and produce squabs, this is not all that is truly desirable. What is wanted is a bird that will produce a large squab of a light color, one that is a good nurse and feeder, and one so prolific that the hen will lay another pair of eggs before the first pair of young are ready to leave the nest. I speak particularly of a light-colored bird because light-colored squabs bring at least twenty-five per cent. more in the market than dark-colored ones, and large, fat squabs are more attractive and salable than small, scrawny ones; and large, fat squabs can only be produced by good feeders and nurses. Consequently such birds are really a necessity and can only be had by carefully selecting and culling, which takes time.

But to make a beginning. If in the neighborhood of a large city you can, by frequently visiting the markets and bird stores, find just what is wanted for your purpose at a low price, and first cost has much to do with the profits of the business. Commission men and dealers are continually receiving consignments of pigeons, and in all these lots you will generally find some large, light-colored, cross-bred birds which will answer your purpose, and, by paying a trifle above the market price, you will be allowed to select from the lot.

Some writers specify a particular variety as being most desirable, such as Duchesse, Antwerps and Dragoons. But my experience teaches me that crosses of these varieties among themselves, or with large common pigeons make the best breeders, and it is just such birds as these that you want to look for in the markets and among the dealers. The one objection to this course is the inability to tell the sex of a bird at sight, but by putting them into a room together you can soon tell male from female, and if you find you have an excess of males, which is generally the case, you can cull them out and either dispose of them or hold them until you procure mates for them. Such a course as this takes time, but all this while you are learning the nature and habits of your birds, and it is better, say, to begin with such a lot of birds which may cost you $1 a pair than to purchase Duchesse, Dragoons and Antwerps at $2 to $3 a pair from breeders at a distance and then not be sure of their being pairs.

If you, after a time, collect a lot of large, light-colored common hens, then it would be well to cross these with Silver, Silver Dun, or White Antwerps, or with Yellow or White Dragoon males; such matings would be likely to bring you large, light-colored squabs. The Duchesse is a large-bodied bird and when pure-bred has feathered or booted legs, which is an objection, as in squab raising a clean-legged bird is most desirable. By crossing a Duchesse hen with a strong

Antwerp or Dragoon male you will get a bird of large body and thinly feathered on legs. Such a bird again crossed with the Dragoon would give just about what is wanted in a squab breeder—a good-sized bird with clean legs. In mating birds for this purpose it is best to have the hen the larger of the pair and yet there should not be too great a disparity in their size.

Many novices, knowing that the Runt is a large pigeon, say at once, "Why that is the pigeon for squabs". In theory this is all right, but from the fact that the Runt is not a prolific bird and that they are not the best of nurses, from a practical point of view this is all wrong. Their squabs are large, but there are not enough of them through the year to satisfy the breeder for market. Then again, large Runts are worth from $8 to $10 a pair, which makes them too expensive even if practical for the purpose.

If these extremely large squabs could be had in sufficient numbers it is a question if, under existing market conditions, they would prove profitable. As squabs are usally sold by the dozen, and not by weight, and the consumption of food by these large birds is twice that consumed by the Duchesse and the Dragoon cross, the expense of keeping the breeding stock and raising the squabs is naturally increased, and the question is, would the price advance in proportion to size and cost? I think not, and consequently this also would be an objection to the Runt for market purposes.

There is a large, white pigeon, frequently met with, by some called a Runt, although not half as large as a true Runt, that would make a good cross with the Dragoon or Antwerp. Those I have frequently seen in the markets of Philadelphia and New York, and when seen always secured them for this purpose. But the intending breeder may not have the advantages of these city markets; in such a case watch the advertisements of the various poultry and pigeon papers and magazines, and what is better advertise for what you want. Then on finding what is wanted make the best bargain possible, either for the lot, for the hens alone, or for pairs. Pigeons at least a year old are the best to begin with, as they are then of the proper age to go right to work, and as the hens are good for four or five years, and the males twice as long, once the flock is established it will need only occasional additions to keep it intact.

While establishing your flock, you must expect many disappointments, especially regarding the sex of those you buy, and if you get a good flock in working order the first year you should be satisfied. After this, by watching your birds you will find which are your best breeders and feeders, and can cull out the poor ones and substitute others at your leisure, as the dairyman does his cows.

The advantage of having all white birds in your flock is that they will always command a good price, when in good plumage, from taxidermists; and so when culling, instead of having to accept the low price that colored pigeons would bring, you can often get all you have paid. To be in good feather the white birds need to be in full feather about the head and throat. Wing-feathers and tail-feathers can be supplied by the stuffer, but only nature and good condition can supply the fine short feathers of the head and throat.

If the intending breeder lives in the country where his birds can fly at liberty, he could keep a flock on purpose to breed squab raisers, and not be obliged to look elsewhere for them. By judicious selection and pairing in a few years a flock could be secured that

BLUE CHECK HOMER.

would make ideal squab raisers. This is no theory, but the actual practice of successful breeders and only needs to be tried to prove its value. As the object is to raise as many young from a pair each year as possible, as soon as it is found that a hen begins to lay only one egg, or is irregular in her laying, it is best to dispose of the pair altogether, or if the mate is a good, strong, healthy bird secure a new partner for him. By having an extra flock to draw from it is an easy matter to keep the breeding stock up to the standard of production desired.

Always have birds mated when turned into the breeding room, and by securing them in a spare breeding space by the wire door before mentioned, they can readily be wonted to a locality. Never allow old cocks nor hens to be flying about; if you do you will find it creating discord, and dividing pairs. Harmony and peace are very necessary factors to success in this line of business. You want no drones, only active workers.

There is often difficulty in determining the sex of pigeons, especially young birds, for nature has not made such a marked difference in the **Distinguishing Sex.** male and female of the genus *Columba* as she has in that of the gallinaceous family. There are various plans given to decide the sex, such as examining the bones of the *os sacrum* or vent; taking the beak of the pigeon in one hand and the feet in the other and stretching them out, if the bird throws its tail it is decided to be a hen, if it hugs it down tightly, a male. In examining the vent, if the breast-bone is short and the bones of the vent wide apart it is declared to be a hen, if close together and the space between them small it is called a male.

I have in years of experience found all these signs

to fail, but if I should lean towards confidence in either one, it would be towards the one depending on the elevation and lowering of the tail. The only sure way I know of is to watch their actions. It will be found the male does most of the cooing, is the more active, and has a little coarser appearance about the head then the hen. If you see one of a flock rather fine about the head, quiet in its actions, and rather inclined to keep out of trouble than fight back, you can reasonably select it as a hen. Try the stretching test and if favored by this test take it as a hen. Place it with one you know to be a cock in a mating-pen, and if old enough to mate you can soon decide as to sex.

I regard a mating-pen ,which is a box with two

FIG. 12.

apartments separated by a wire partition as shown in Fig. 12, so that the birds you desire to pair can see each other between the wires, a very necessary addition to every breeding loft. By placing all uncertain birds in this before turning them into the breeding room, you can be sure that they are safe to trust together alone. If in a promiscuous lot of pigeons you find one bird following another about from place to place and occasionally pecking at it, you can be sure that this is a mated pair, and that the cock is, as it is termed, driving, the hen to nest. If it is about time for her to lay she will soon settle in the nest selected for her and her mate will be satisfied, but if she is not ready to lay, the cock may drive her too hard and abuse her: in such a case they should be separated.

FOOD AND FEEDING.

—

T HE kinds of food, and time to feed, are matters of necessary consideration; to choose food that will be relished, and to so vary it as to keep the birds in good appetite and condition. For a breeding bird that eats but little will make a poor feeder and your young stock will suffer accordingly. The idea is to keep a bird that has a good appetite and pays strict attention to the care of its young, from getting cloyed or getting too fat and lazy.

All food should be placed in a covered feed-box or trough as shown in Fig. 13. To make one take an inch board ten inches wide and six feet long, make sides and ends of strips two and one-half inches wide, nailed to upper side of this board; make a corresponding frame of same size, and attach a hinged cover to it; connect the two by strips of lathes nine inches long, placed two inches apart, and you have a covered feed-box that the pigeons cannot get into, and from which they cannot throw out the grain. As many of these can be made as is necessary to accommodate the birds you have to feed, allowing one to every twenty-five or thirty pairs of birds. By having feed-box covered they cannot soil the grain and through spaces made by the slats every bird can feed without interruption from its neighbor. When small flocks are kept a galvanized iron hopper, as shown in Fig. 14, is splendid for keep-

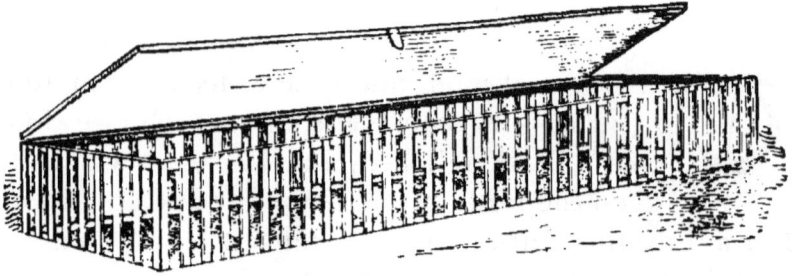

FIG. 13.

ing the feed in. Such a hopper avoids waste and au-
tomatically lets the grain down as used.

As economy in food is one great item in this business, it is a point to be well considered. But the cheapest food is not always the most economical. To buy
grain that has been wet, and run the chances of its being musty is unsafe, for musty grain is sure to produce
disease of throat and bowels. Rye is not a safe food;
unhulled oats are bad. New wheat and new corn are
both productive of bowel trouble. Screening, if dry,

FIG. 14

sweet, and of first quality are
to be recommended, but what
is known and sold as screenings is usually full of chess,
cockle, rye, and blasted grain,
and is in no sense an economical food. In truth the best,
safest, and most satisfactory
food for all times and seasons
is good, sound, dry red wheat
(never white wheat) and sound
cracked corn. These should
not be mixed, but fed sepa-
rately, say three feeds of wheat and then a feed of
cracked corn, making the change from one to the other
as far as possible in the morning when crops are empty.

Wheat can be bought in quantity when cheap and kept in a dry place, but cracked corn should only be bought or prepared in small quantities at a time, as it absorbs moisture quickly, and if kept in large quantities is apt to mould and become musty and sour.

This food can be varied with occasional feeds of buckwheat, millet, and Canada peas, if prices are not too high. Hemp seed should always be kept on hand for sick or debilitated birds, and once a month give a feed of hemp seed to all. Pigeons are very fond of this seed, but it is too heating and stimulating for a general food. Good, sound hulled oats also makes a good food for a change, and dried stale bread crushed fine, mixed with bran and a very little salt and moistened makes an economical food and one that is greatly relished. No green food is necessary at any time, although lettuce is sometimes given—nothing else, however.

In feeding birds much food is frequently wasted by giving more at one time than the birds will clean up. Birds feeding their young should be fed twice each day; the first time as soon after daylight as possible, the second time about three o'clock in the afternoon, in the Winter, and four in the Summer, thus giving the old birds time to fill the crops of their young before dark. Only as much feed should be given each time as the birds will clean up. This amount can be readily ascertained by measuring the amount in a bucket for a few times. If at the next feeding there still remains some of the preceding feeding, reduce the amount until just what is nicely cleaned up is used.

Of course, the same number of birds will eat considerably more at one time of the month than another, depending on the number of squabs they are feeding.

But by giving it close attention the feeder can calculate about what will be consumed. If much food is left when birds have been feeding as a general thing liberally, you may have a suspicion that all is not right, and instead of turning fresh food in with that which is left, remove it altogether, sift it and examine it, and watch the results of the food supplied in its place; if that is again refused you may know there is something that has made it distasteful and other food should be substituted. For this reason it is not always safe to buy too large a quantity of grain at once, until it is found to be satisfactory to your birds.

In addition to the feed-boxes, provide some low boxes as shown in Fig. 15, in which to keep a supply of grit or gravel, also ground oyster shells. At the present time there are various kinds of prepared grit offered for sale, but, if convenient to a

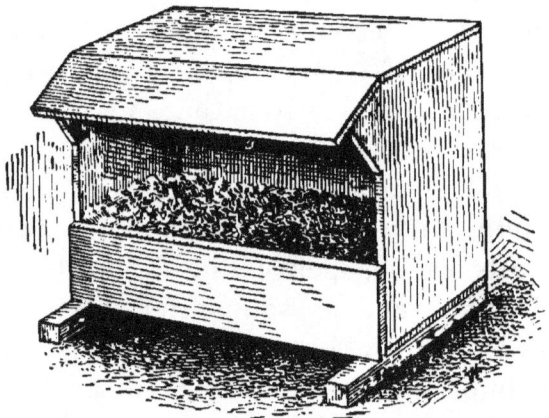

FIG. 15.

shore of ocean, lake, or pond you can with a sieve and a little labor get all the grit you need. A box of broken bone and broken charcoal while not a necessity will be found to be acceptable to the birds. Old lime mortar such as comes from stone or brick walls, especially if wet with a little stale urine, will be found to be often visited. Pigeons have such a liking for this, that they will, if confined in a brick building, peck it out from between the bricks. When put in a box it needs to be broken into small pieces and not left in the lump.

Pigeons should have at all times an abundance of fresh, clean water both for bathing and drinking pur-

Water. poses. If it can be supplied from a source that can furnish constantly a running supply, so much the better, as nothing has a tendency to create disease like impure water, and water kept in open vessels is sure to be fouled after standing a few hours. Water even in closed vessels becomes impure if it stands over twenty-four hours. Consequently the water supply needs very careful attention. If running water can be supplied, it can be conducted through the breeding rooms in a long, narrow trough, say six inches wide and three inches deep, so arranged at the waste end as not to clog and overflow; or it can be

FIG. 16.

run into small tanks or boxes, two feet by four feet from four to five inches deep. In such a tank the pigeons can also bathe at will and the constant flow of water keeps the tank free from impurities with the assistance of a daily cleansing. But if no facilities for running water exist then recourse must be had to fountains, as shown in Figs. 16 and 17, of which there are many patterns. The former is made of galvanized

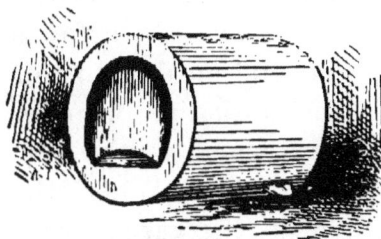

FIG. 17.

iron, and the latter of earthen-ware. Both of these fountains are automatic and keep the water pure and cool. They are made in various sizes. These are better than open tubs, because the water can be kept cooler and purer than in open vessels, and by having a number placed at different points about the loft accommodations can be had for all. Those who have had experience with open tubs know how common it is for pigeons, especially in Summer time, to crowd into a freshly filled tub and take a

FIG. 18.

bath, leaving the water of a milky hue from the impurities of their bodies. While this may in time settle, the impurities remain until the tub is emptied and scrubbed out, and for birds to be obliged to drink such water is certainly not conducive to health. If an open pan is used to supply water for drinking purposes, a wire frame like that shown in Fig. 18 should be made around it to keep the birds from getting into and fouling the water.

A bath two or three times a week is a necessity for perfect health, as this is the only way pigeons have of ridding themselves of vermin and cleansing their feathers and bodies. Gallinaceous birds or fowls depend on dry dust or earth for this purpose, but water is the sole

FIG. 19.

dependence of the Columbarian family. When the weather and temperature permit of it, the yard or area is the best place for the bath, as the splashing that usually follows the birds' entry into the water can do no harm. But when too cold and stormy it must be taken inside, and the water be made luke warm. Tubs suitable for bathing can be made by taking any strongly made barrel, and sawing off the ends, making two tubs about five inches deep, as shown in Fig. 19. Another pattern of bath tub is made like that shown in Fig. 20. This tub is about three feet in length, a foot and a half in width, and five inches deep, lined inside with tin or galvanized iron. These must be emptied and set aside after all have had a chance to bathe. If it is desired to use them for drinking purposes, they can be fitted with a cover, and holes made in this cover, oval in shape, and about four inches wide in the widest part. Then after the bath is taken the tubs can be refilled, the cover put on and birds take the water at will.

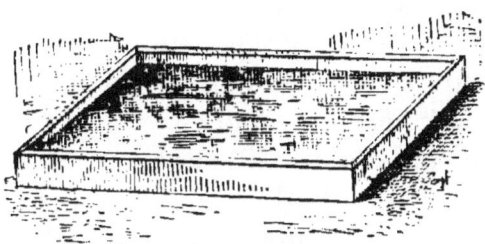

FIG. 20.

Salt is almost as much of a necessity to pigeons as food. Certainly they do not thrive without it, and every good breeder keeps a supply of it where it can be taken at pleasure. The best form to give it is

Salt.

in the lump, as it comes from the quarries, known as mineral or rock salt; a lump will weigh from four to ten pounds and can be purchased at most feed stores. Placed on the floor it gathers moisture from the air and so keeps in a condition that the birds can easily get all that they need. Fine salt would be likely to be too freely partaken of, and be an injury rather than a benefit. If rock salt cannot be obtained take a ten-pound bag of table salt, wet it thoroughly and then bake it in the oven. It will usually bake hard and in this state will take the place of rock salt.

The salt-cat is another necessary compound for the health of pigeons. It is made in various ways but as good a mixture as I know of is brick-maker's loam, sharp sand, and old lime mortar (free from hair) one-half peck each; to this add one-half pound carraway seed, one-half pound coriander, one-half pound cummin seed crushed, and one pint bay salt. Mix it thoroughly together, wetting it with stale urine, until it is of the consistency of stiff mortar. Mould it into cakes three inches thick and six inches in diameter, dry thoroughly in the sun, then place in a small box similar to the one shown in Fig. 15, in the loft, and the pigeons will soon show their appreciation of it. Another formula is, one peck sifted dry loam, one handful or flour, one handful ground cloves, one handful of fennel seed, one handful of dill seed, one handful of cummin seed, one handful of fennigreek, one handful of powdered assafetida, three double handfuls of table salt, one double handful bay salt. Mix well dry, and then add water to make as stiff as putty, divide in three-pound lumps, and bake in oven or dry in the sun.

Pigeons in a state of nature build a rough nest of twigs and coarse grasses. In confinement they are unable to get such material, but as a substitute tobacco

Nesting Material. stems can be used, which not only satisfy the natural desire to build but also answer as a guard against vermin. A few of these placed in one corner of the breeding room occasionally, will be quickly appropriated. Some breeders do not believe in coarse nesting material, and in its place use coarse pine shavings, renewing them as often as they become foul. But this does not satisfy the natural de-

WHITE HOMING PIGEONS.

sire that the pigeon has to build a nest, and so I believe that they should be gratified in this natural instinct, although I also think a layer of coarse pine sawdust for a foundation where nest-pans are not used is a good thing. It prevents the excrement from sticking to the floor of the apartment, is a preventive of lice, and is easily removed and renewed as soon as the young birds are taken away.

It is a question with many as to what is the best material for covering the floor of a breeding room, some advocating sawdust, some sand, and others the new peat mass so much used for bedding for horses. According to my experience, good sharp beach sand is the best, as it is a good absorbent and can be kept clean by raking over once a day, and needs renewing but seldom. If unable to get beach sand, then sawdust is next best on account of its cheapness, but it needs to be placed pretty thickly on the floor, or when dried out it will be blown about by the birds when flying around, leaving bare places on the floor, and gathering in windrows about the sides. This also needs to be raked over daily and the refuse gathered up. The peat mass mentioned is an excellent floor material, being an absorbent and thus preventing any disagreeable odors, but it being expensive puts it out of the reach of the squab raiser who must study economy in all supplies.

All the rakings of the loft and nests should be saved and put into barrels. It all has a value, and is eagerly sought after by gardeners and morocco manufacturers. **Manure.** The freer it is kept from sticks and sawdust the more it is prized, and as this all counts in with the profits it needs some attention. The dung of domestic birds in general contains salts similar to those of guano, and for mulberries, vines peaches, and other fruits and plants, one part of the droppings to from four to ten of water has been found to produce excellent results. To realize the full value of the manure, have a dry house and plenty of good absorbent on the shelves and dropping-boards. Gather twice a week and mix with twice the quantity of good woods earth or dry muck, and keep in barrels in a dry place, or compost them as soon as gathered with twice or three times their bulk of dry material.

Feathers, also, are an item of profit and need to be cared for. All the feathers plucked from the squabs, the old birds that die, and those that gather in the rooms at molting time, should be gathered together, separated from the wing and tail-feathers, thoroughly heated by steam or otherwise, and kept in bags. They will sell at some price and pay for the care given them.

BREEDING AND MANAGEMENT.

EVERY thing in the breeding room being arranged for the comfort and convenience of the birds, and each pair properly mated, they can now be placed in the apartments provided for them, kept there a few days until wonted to their locality, and then given the liberty of the loft or room. If they are properly mated they will soon begin to build their nest and the hen to lay. She usually lays two eggs, a day intervening between the first and second egg. Some breeders advocate removing the first egg and replacing it in the nest when the second is laid, but this is not natural and I believe in letting matters take a natural course. By watching the birds carefully one can readily tell when the eggs are laid, and if each apartment is numbered, the date of laying can be entered in a book kept for the purpose, and then it can be known when they are due to hatch.

The period of incubation is from sixteen to eighteen days, and the cock takes his turn of sitting with the hen, he sitting from ten in the morning to about four in the afternoon, and she, taking his place at that time, continues on through the night until about ten the next morning. After the birds have been sitting three or four days an examination of the eggs will show whether they are fertile or not. Take them in the hand and hold between the eye and a strong light. If fertile they will be dark and opaque. If infertile they will be clear and nearly transparent. Sometimes one egg will be fertile, and the other clear. If you have kept the date that the eggs were laid, and have two pairs that have had eggs close together, and both with one fertile egg and one clear, one pair can be broken up, and their egg given to the other pair, and in a week or so the pair that has been left without eggs will be ready to lay again. Never give one pair of birds three eggs, because two young birds are all, really, that an old pair can feed properly, and to divide the care between three that should be given only to two will result in all three being under size, and is poor economy.

If a hen sits her full time, and at the end of the eighteenth day there are no young, the eggs might as

PEEPER, ONE DAY OLD.

well be taken from the pair, as it is only a waste of time to allow them to sit longer. The young often die in the shell from chill, or other unknown causes, a week before the time for hatching comes around. Careful observation and experience will teach the breeder to tell about this time whether there is still life in the egg, by holding it between the eye and a strong light, and if all life seems to be extinct take such eggs away. If one egg only is bad the pair should be permitted to hatch the fertile egg, and then after the young bird is a week old, and the old birds have fed off their soft food, this young bird can be transferred to some other pair that has only one young. Make the transfer to the pair that are known to be the best feeders.

The soft food mentioned is a peculiar condition that the food taken by the parent bird assumes about the time the eggs are ready to hatch. All food taken changes to a chymey nature, and is known as pigeon's milk. This wonderful provision of nature for the sustenance of the little morsel that is released from the egg at the end of the incubating period, blind and helpless, enables the parent bird to give it nourishment until it is able to take whole grain. To feed it the old bird takes the bill of the young one in its mouth, and, by a spasmodic action of crop and throat, injects the "milk" into the mouth of the younger bird. This is kept up for some time, and gradually mixed with grain taken by the parent, until finally the grain is taken whole, simply being moistened in the o'd bird's crop. After this milky change in the food takes place, it is necessary for the health of the old birds that it should be "fed off" and this is why no change of young is advised at

SQUEAKERS, TEN DAYS OLD.

once. Pigeons losing their young from any cause before this soft-food period is past are frequently made sick. So much so as to interfere with their immediate laying. Consequently the breeder needs to pay attention to this time, and if he finds the young of a pair dead, he should then borrow one from another pair, about the same age, which they can feed, until the danger is passed, when it can be returned to the original nest. Experience will teach any one how to make these changes so that they shall keep the stock increasing.

SQUEALERS, THREE WEEKS OLD.

Frequently a pair will build, and although they go to nest, and perform all the duties of a mated pair, there will be no eggs. This proves that the hen is either not well matured, or barren. Such a pair if given a pair of fertile eggs will likely sit on them, hatch them, and care well for the young, and often the natural functions of the hen are aroused and she will commence laying, as she is expected to do. If after raising a pair of young, the hen still neglects to lay, you can count her as barren, and of no use, and she should be cast aside and the male provided with a new mate.

Often where there are two squabs in a nest, one will seem to get the greater part of the food, and be plump and thrifty, while the other is puny and starved. Why it is that the old birds seem to favor one more than the other no one can explain, but the fact remains. The way to do in such cases is either to transfer the weaker bird to a pair with a single bird about its size, or to feed it by hand. To feed by hand soak the grain you feed in water, until soft, and then feed a grain at a time until the little crop is filled, or take pellets of moist bread and feed in the same way. Some breeders take the grain in their mouth, chew it fine, and then by inserting the squab's bill between the lips, by the aid of the tongue force the food into the squab's mouth. A little practice will enable one to feed very quickly, and the young bird learns to take it as readily, and manifests its eagerness to be fed whenever its feeder approaches the nest. Such an operation may not at first strike any one favorably, but on learning how, many squabs can be saved and raised by this process, and putting it in practice one's squeamishness is overcome and the practice found to be not such a disagreeable one as at first supposed. After feeding in this way a few days and getting the neglected bird in good condition, the old birds will be likely to pay it more attention and feed it as they are expected to do.

Cleanliness and quiet are very essential to success in this business, consequently you want few visitors and no disturbing influences. If you find some pairs in your lot that appear to be quarrelsome, better remove them and substitute others, for they will do more harm than good, even though they may raise a few squabs themselves. The floors should be raked over every day, and the offal gathered up and saved. When a pair has done with one nest clean it out thoroughly, and put in fresh sawdust. If you can get cedar saw-dust it is better than pine. Watch closely for lice, es-

pecially during the Summer, and if you see any indi-
cations around the cracks of the partitions or elsewhere, give them a dose of kerosene oil; this will
quickly dispose of them. By having a squirt-can you
can easily inject the oil into any crack or opening, and
it is sure death to insect life, while the odor does not
seem to have any bad effect on the pigeons.

Move quietly about the room and your birds will
soon learn to know you and have no fear of you.

DRESSING SQUABS FOR MARKET.

IN dressing squabs for market it is important to kill them at about the time they have reached the best market condition, which is just about four weeks as a rule, although some parents will feed their young better than others, and in twenty-five days have them as forward as they would be in twenty-eight days under other care. But while four weeks is about the usual time, if not well developed, that is, if the abdomen has not become firm and hard, they had better be left a week longer, and such birds will be found to have gained more in that additional time. After a little practice the breeder can tell, almost at a glance, whether the squab is in proper condition to kill. What is wanted is large, fat squabs, and about the time they start to leave the nest is the time they attain this condition. A careful supervision will enable one to tell what pairs have their young in proper condition.

They should be collected the afternoon of the day before they are to be killed, and put in boxes, so that their crops will be emptied of all food at the time of killing. This is important, as the birds look bad and do not keep so well if food is left in their crops after being killed. But the crop can be emptied by squeezing out the grain with the fingers, in case it is not possible to collect all you want to ship the day before, but this adds much to the work and should be avoided if possible.

When ready to kill take the squab in the left hand, holding the wings and the feet together in a firm grasp, the head between the thumb and fore-finger, then insert the blade of a sharp penknife into the mouth, sever the jugular vein at the back of the head, drop the head and the blood will readily flow out of the mouth. As soon as the blood has ceased to flow, commence plucking the feathers, beginning with those of head and tail, as birds pick easier at this time than at any other, everything seeming to relax, and for this reason squabs should only be killed as they are wanted for picking. Take only a few feathers at a time so as to avoid tearing the skin. It is tedious business at first, but practice will soon make perfect. Even the most expert will, once in a while, tear the skin, it is so tender, but as far as possible it must be avoided, as it injures the appearance of the squab, and detracts from its selling qualities. A good picker will pick from seven to eight pairs an hour. Some have a record as high as twelve and fourteen, but very few can work as fast as this, and seven pairs an hour is considered good work.

After the squab is picked clean, throw it into cold water, slightly salted, and leave it in about thirty minutes. This takes out the animal heat, plumps them up, and makes them appear lighter colored than if left as they come from the picker. When the half-hour is up, take them from the water, wash all dirt from their feet, and blood from their mouth and head, fold the wings nicely across the back, tie the two inside legs together of a pair, always putting squabs of same size and fatness together, and they are ready for packing.

PAIR BLUE DRAGOONS.

When ready to ship squabs to market, divide them up in the box or boxes, so that all the largest and finest lay together on the top of the box, **Shipping and Selling.** and all the poorest at the bottom. If your stock is properly looked after there will not be many poor ones. In cold weather, it is only necessary to pack in neat, strong boxes, in layers, breast down. Six layers is enough, as too many are apt to flatten down and take away that plump, round appearance, that goes so far toward making them attractive and salable at good prices. The boxes should not be tight, but open just enough to let a little air in. In Summer put a good layer of ice in the bottom of the box, then put in your squabs, and on top of them, for the last layer, put cracked ice again. The ice melting and the water trickling down between the birds keeps them nice and cool until they get to their destination. Naturally the box for Summer use needs to be tighter than that for cold weather.

In looking for purchasers for squabs you will find, if you can give a steady supply week after week, there will be no difficulty in obtaining the best class of customers—private parties, hotels, and fine restaurants. Make the best arrangements you can with them as to prices and number they will take for the season, and then aim to retain their custom by supplying only the best. All game stores handle squabs, but the best paying trade is private families, who will take one or two pairs every week the year round and at a fair price. In the markets you can also sell at all times but not at such good figures. Try to get every private family you can, as you get the best retail price from them. Find out what they have paid and what they will pay and arrange accordingly. If you live so far from a large city that you can not look up your customers, it would often pay to advertise that families will be supplied on demand. Or you could consign your stock to a good, reliable commission house, which will often obtain very fair prices for you. The best location, however, for a squab raiser is near enough to a large city to be able to get in once a week, to look after sales, customers, and other details. If you have only a few pairs each week, they can easily be put in a canvas case or basket and carried along with you as desired.

As to selling price, that depends on the size and condition of squabs, and season of the year, from the poorest, thin little things in Mid-summer at twenty cents a pair (that no man who pretends to raise squabs for profit would ever send to market) to the extra large fat squabs, that retail in Mid-winter all the way up to $1 a pair. Of course, wholesale prices would be from ten to twenty per cent. less than these prices, on the same birds. A successful squab raiser ought to be able to retail squabs at an average of sixty cents a pair the year round. This is for strictly first-class birds. What few second-grade squabs he would have to sell ought to average forty cents per pair the year through, but these last should be very few in number only from young breeders.

With good management a good pair of breeders ought, at a low calculation, to clear $1 a year, often more, seldom less. The manure and feathers when properly cared for will raise this average five to ten cents a pair, so that if you have five hundred breeding pairs, you could reasonably expect to realize a profit of at least $500 a year, or $1,000 on one thousand pairs, and in that ratio according to the number of pairs you keep.

Good breeders will lay from six to eight pairs of eggs a year, but it is very few that will hatch all the eggs, or raise all the young that are hatched. If they would all do this, there would be few better paying investments. The estimate of profit made does not include cost of labor.

To conclude, any one who decides to embark in the business of squab raising must conduct it on business methods, giving it personal attention, having regular times for feeding, cleaning, and collecting the squabs, learning the peculiarities of his birds, and treating them so as to gain their confidence, discarding such as prove quarrelsome or bad nurses, and watching at all times for opportunities to secure stock that shall give size and quality to his flock. Experience will teach him many lessons not contained in this little book, but if what has been written proves of benefit to the reader, the object aimed at, that of aiding the beginner in his first endeavors in squab raising, will have been accomplished and the book have fulfilled its mission.

DISEASES OF PIGEONS.

NO matter how careful you may be, in all collections of pigeons, especially large ones, there will be some that suffer from the diseases peculiar to the species. Of these I can only speak in a general way and treat of the most common, for it does not pay a squab breeder to devote much time to the sick. It is better to remove them at once, and replace them with others, for even if cured it may be a long time before they get into good breeding condition again, and the time and attention given them could more profitably be given to the well. Among the most common ailments are canker, cholera, egg bound, enteritis, going light, roup, small pox, sudden colds, wing disease, and worms.

Canker is an evil that the squab raiser has sometimes to contend with. The cause of it is often ascribed to impure air and water, but as it makes its **Canker.** appearance in flocks that have the best of care, this evidently is not the true cause. It is diphtheritic in its nature, and the symptoms are high fever, congestion, and swelling of the blood-vessels of the throat, accompanied by little white ulcers, which, if neglected, spread very rapidly all over the interior of the mouth and throat. Like roup it usually makes its appearance in cold, damp weather. When a squab once becomes affected old and young should be at once taken from the breeding room and the apartment they occupied disinfected. The old birds should be examined, and if found with canker in their mouths it should be removed and the canker spots painted with a solution of lemon juice and sugar. Powdered burnt alum is also good to apply. The young birds can be treated in the same way, but if the canker has spread much about the mouth it hardly pays to spend much time over them. The old birds need to be thoroughly cured before turning back into the breeding room. A small piece of alum in the drinking water of the old birds will aid in the cure, and if the whole flock is threatened a piece in the different drinking vessels for awhile will act as a preventive.

Cholera. Cholera usually attacks pigeons in hot weather, and can generally be attributed to improper food, new wheat, musty corn, foul screenings, or impure water. It is accompanied by a watery diarrhea of a greenish color. The plumage is dull and the bird mopes and soon loses its strength. Change its food and place a little prepared chalk in the water. I have found a lump of quick lime about the size of a walnut placed in a two-gallon vessel of water to be a check to the discharges.

Egg Bound. Hens, especially young ones, often have trouble in voiding or passing their eggs. Frequently the first egg will be voided all right, and the hen on the following day give evidence of distress sometimes entirely losing the use of her legs and unable to stand. By taking her in the hands, and feeling of the abdomen, the egg can generally be located, and when convinced that this is the cause of the trouble nature needs to be assisted. One way to do this is after rubbing the passage with vaseline or sweet oil, introducing the finger as far as possible, at the same time being careful not to break the egg, holding her abdomen over steam, not so hot as to scald, but so as to thoroughly warm and relax the parts as much as possible. After a few minutes of such treatment as this, put her in a quiet pen and unless a very stubborn case she will soon pass the egg. Some at the same time as treating with the steam, give the hen a small quantity of molasses internally.

Inflammation of the bowels, or enteritis as it is called, is the result of a chill and the symptoms are a **Enteritis.** "puffed-up" condition of the feathers, moping, and a bloody discharge of mucus. Place the bird in a warm place and give a few drops of paregoric two or three times a day.

"Going light," the term used among pigeon fanciers for atrophy or wasting, is a condition in which the bird gradually grows thinner and thinner, and is a form of consumption. While I do not consider it contagious, it is best to remove the sufferer from the rest, for no **"Going Light."** bird with any form of disease should be allowed to remain in the breeding room. It is usually accompanied by diarrhea, the discharges clinging to the vent, fouling the plumage and presenting a disgusting appearance. If you see a bird with its plumage discolored, its motions uncertain, its eye dull, catch it, and you can soon determine by feeling of it, whether it is "going light" or not; for its breast-bone will be prominent and its natural plumpness gone if affected by this disease. I have found an almost certain remedy, if taken in the early stages, to be plucking out its entire tail. Then by using one or two cod liver oil capsules and a grain of quinine daily, and feeding a little hemp seed with its other food, it will, by the time its

tail has grown again, be entirely recovered. But it
will be a long time if a hen before she will be in laying
condition, and the question naturally arises, is it
profitable to wait for recovery and also give the time
necessary to attend to it while sick ?

Roup. Roup is a disease of a catarrhal nature, affecting the
mucous membranes of the nostrils, head, and throat,
and is usually accompanied by a profuse discharge of sticky mucous matter from the nostrils, which, if the disease is neglected, become very
offensive. It is very contagious, and should be check-
ed as soon as it makes its appearance by removing the
sufferers to a distance, as if left to fly around they
would soon contaminate the most of the flock. It
seems to be miasmatic in its nature, as it makes its appearance suddenly, sometimes affecting a number at
once, and when they have been in no way exposed to
its influence. Sudden changes of temperature with
damp and chilly conditions are particularly favorable
to its appearance. On the first indication of difficult
breathing give a pill, about the size of a medium-sized
pea, of butter and black pepper, equal parts, and swab
the throat with a solution of chlorate of potash.
Should there be a discharge of mucus, wash the nostrils and inside of the mouth with a solution of perox-
ide of hydrogen ; this is said to be a sovereign remedy
for roup. Dry quarters, protection from draughts, and
an occasional use of a disinfectant will do much to keep
this scourge at bay.

Small Pox. A disease that sometimes makes its appearance in
large flocks of pigeons, and quite contagious, is known
as small pox. It comes in the form of
small sores about the head, and if left to
take its course spreads over the head and neck, form-

ing one large mass of scabby sores. On its first appearance isolate the afflicted ones, and touch the sores with a solution of blue vitriol. A few applications will generally check its tendency to spread.

In cases of sudden cold, or where a tonic seems to be necessary, a one-grain pill of quinine, and a capsule of cod liver oil, given twice a day, will be found to have

Sudden Colds. good results. Especially is this the case during the molting season where a bird does not seem to shed well and is drooping. It is a trying time for all pigeons and unless in robust health the process will be slow. As they do not usually breed while molting, it is an advantage to have it over as soon as possible, and consequently pigeons should be kept in good, healthy condition and encouraged to shed as rapidly as is consistent with good health. A little stimulating food, such as hemp and canary seed, is good at such times.

Wing disease is a stiffening of the joints of the wings, caused by the formation of a tumor at this point,

Wing Disease. and no doubt arises from a strain, or injury by a blow. It first appears as a small, inflamed spot, and if neglected, grows larger and larger, until finally it hardens, fills with a yellow cheesy matter, which after a time breaks the skin and protrudes, increasing in size daily, until it eventually weakens the bird so much that it dies. If you notice one of your birds that seems to have difficulty in flying, and drags one wing on the ground, examine it and you will, no doubt, find the wing-joint inflamed. Place it in the hospital that should be attached to every breeding-house, rub it well with strong spirits of camphor twice daily, or paint with iodine, and you will, if you have discovered it in time, no doubt effect a cure.

Sometimes even though you may relieve the inflammation and apparently cure the disease, the wing will remain stiff. This, while it renders the bird in a measure helpless and unsightly, does not injure it as a breeder, for it will still continue to lay, sit, and feed; but on account of its being unable to fly it must, of necessity, make its nest on the floor.

Worms sometimes prove troublesome to pigeons. The pigeon has a varying appetite, and while it may **Worms.** seem to eat and drink, does not appear to be doing well. If watched carefully the worms will appear in their dung, and when it is determined that this is the cause, give a piece of garlic about the size of a medium white bean every morning, and watch the results; or a small pill of powdered areca nut and butter, for two or three days, followed by a capsule of castor oil. I have always found the garlic to be an effective cure. A small piece of gum aloes, about the size of a Canada pea, will also be found effective, all to be given before the bird is fed in the morning.

What is known as the Douglass Mixture added to the drinking water, in proportion of a tablespoonful **Douglass Mixture.** to a pint of water, is a good tonic for all times. The mixture is made by dissolving one-half pound of green copperas in two gallons of water, adding to it one ounce of sulphuric acid. This, if placed in the drinking vessels occasionally during the molting season, will be found to assist molting and keep the strength of the bird from diminishing.

Part II.

INTRODUCTORY.

HAVING felt the need of proper advice for the successful breeding of squabs for market, and knowing that hundreds of others like myself have suffered loss and disappointment in their first efforts, have prompted me to write these hints.

Squab raising is, when properly managed, undoubtedly one of the best paying businesses that can be started with a comparatively small capital; the percentage of profit on the capital invested is very large, everything being considered. It can be carried on in connection with the poultry business very nicely. The care and housing of pigeons and poultry differ considerably. A larger number of pigeons can be raised successfully on the same amount of ground than chickens.

The following remarks are based entirely on personal experience as well as that of others who are engaged largely in the business in this section of the country, (vicinity of Philadelphia.) A much longer account might have been written, but life is short and the getting at the main points of most value to the breeder in the briefest possible way has been my chief aim, and I recommended this work to all intending breeders of squabs, hoping that it will be of material benefit and be the instrument of assisting them to success.

G. H. BRINTON.

MONEY IN SQUABS.

THERE are many different styles of lofts and houses, but I have come to the conclusion that the one best adapted for the purpose is the one described below. Houses for raising squabs should always be built on the ground, as considerable time and labor will be saved in feeding and watering; besides, I am of the opinion that birds thrive better when they are on the ground than when confined exclusively to the loft or an elevated avairy.

Breeding Houses. The house is easier to clean and the expense is less than if the house were built two stories high. If one has room in a barn loft and no place else, it is, of course, possible to raise good squabs there, but whenever possible I would advise the house be built on the ground; especially is this the case when large numbers of birds are kept. The carrying of water and feed up one or more flights of stairs at feeding time is laborious.

To construct a breeding-house, procure good hemlock sheathing boards, twelve inches wide, sixteen feet long, and one inch thick. Use two by four hemlock scantling, sixteen feet long, and the cheapest matched flooring. The building should stand seven feet at rear in the clear, inside, and eight feet at the front, inside, and should be fifteen feet from front to rear, over all. Straight sides and ends, roof slanting one foot from front to rear. The front should have three by six feet windows, at intervals of six or eight feet, extending to within one foot of the floor. This will give light when the birds are confined to the house on account of inclement weather. All windows should be made to slide sideways inside the building, and should be kept open in hot weather. The house should face the south, or south-east. Such a house may be extended indefinitely to accommodate the number of birds to be kept.

A house fifteen feet square would hold comfortably seventy-five pairs of birds. In front of the house should be the wire-netted run or aviary, extending twenty to thirty feet deep and eight feet high. A bottom board twelve inches wide should extend around the enclosure and light lumber should be used for the balance of the framework, with as few posts as possible for center supports. Around the run, about six feet from the ground, six-inch fence boards should be placed for walks or perches for the birds. They should have free flight through the center of the run as much as possible. One-inch mesh is the best to use, as it will keep out rats and English sparrows. The door to the squab-house should be wide enough for a wheelbarrow to be gotten through to remove the manure, etc. The opening for the birds to get into the aviary should be in the center of the building, about four feet from the ground, and should be about six inches wide, six feet long, with a drop-board same size hung on pulleys, or so arranged that it can easily be raised or lowered at will by cords extending to the outside of the wire run, so that the drop can be let down at night without going into the building. There are always some birds in a large flock that are wild and fly into the yard the moment they hear the door open.

WHITE DUCHESSE.

A perch about eight or ten inches wide should extend along the whole bottom of the opening, on which the birds may alight. Tin or sheet iron, covering a space of two feet below the opening and a foot above, and extending a foot on either end, will prevent mice and rats from entering easily, as they have difficulty in obtaining a foot-hold on the tin. The house and roof should be thoroughly covered with two-ply tar roofing paper, well put on and covered with slag cement. The front of the house, facing the yards, may be weather-stripped and painted, if preferred. It is very important to give the tar paper the coating of slag cement as soon as put on, to protect it from the action of the weather. A coat of slag (tar) cement over the building, put on once a year, will preserve it for years in good condition. All doors should have spring hinges so that they will keep shut when not in use. Along the front of the house, about eight feet apart and two feet below the roof, cut out with compass saw a board one foot square, saw the top across, then nail on stout pieces of boot or other leather for hinges, then saw bottom and sides, and you have a small swinging-door ventilator to be used only in hot weather. Tack on some wire netting inside, so that the birds will not fly in and out, and during hot weather these ventilators will prove of great advantage. In Winter these ventilating doors should be nailed shut and a piece of heavy paper tacked over the inside to prevent draughts.

Having described the outside of the breeding-house and the yard, we will now look to the arrangement of the interior. When you enter from the outside door you should have a small wire partition separating a small room from the main room, to be used as a feed-room. In a building fifteen by forty feet, a space three feet wide would be sufficient. In this apartment is stored in barrels the feed, salt, oyster shell, grit, tobacco stems, squab boxes, baskets, tools, etc., ready for immediate use. In a small house it would not be necessary to have this space, as the barrels could be set in any convenient space inside, but when from three to five thousand birds are kept, it is, of course, necessary to have the stores near at hand and convenient to use. When a large number of birds are kept, a small room about fifteen feet square with a stove in, should be attached to the house for use in picking squabs and for storage. Directly facing the outside door should be the door leading from the feed-room into the nesting-room, so that a barrow may be wheeled from one room to another. The nesting-room in a house fifteen feet wide may be any length up to say forty feet, which should accommodate about three or four hundred pairs of birds. If the house be one hundred and twenty feet long, it should be divided into three or more apartments, wire netting partitions being all that is necessary to separate the rooms. Spring doors should be used in each of the partitions. The room should be lined with nesting-boxes, excepting where the doors, windows and ventilators are, the nests to extend from the floor upward six feet, making five nests in each division, as the floor is not intended to be used to nest on, although the birds will occasionally use it for that purpose.

The nest-boxes are made by erecting twelve-inch wide boards, six feet high, set on ends, leaving a space of twelve inches between each two boards, all around the whole room, excepting at windows, etc., as before mentioned. These boards are secured at the bottom by nailing to the floor and at the top by laying a twelve-inch board over all, making a walk on top for the pigeons. Then take twelve-inch boards and cut off in pieces one foot square, five for each division in the house; in a forty-foot house, allowing for windows, etc., it would take about three hundred and fifty pieces, which makes about three hundred and fifty nests to a forty-foot house, accommodating three hundred pairs of birds. Having the three hundred and fifty pieces of board, one foot square, next cut from three-inch stripping three hundred and fifty pieces, twelve inches long, and nail these pieces to each piece of twelve-inch board; nail to the side of the board, at the end, so that the two boards together, representing the bottom of the nest, will be twelve inches square one way and four by twelve inch end, that is, the three-inch stripping and one inch of end of board. A lot of stripping one inch square, or one-inch-square pickets may be used. These should be cut up into twelve-inch lengths and nailed to the sides of the divisions as cleats, commencing about one foot above the floor and leaving about eleven inches between each piece on the division board. In this way five sets of strips are put in each division; the nest-boards will then slide in, resting in these cleats like a drawer. Each nest can readily be lifted out to be cleaned or changed at any time. All nests should be interchangeable so that it does not matter if the same one is not put back. This is, I consider, by far the best arrangement for breeding nests that is in use at the present time. Many advocate the use of nest-pans, etc. I have used several different kinds, but I find nothing is so good in the long run as these board nest-boxes, besides being more economical, a very important point to most breeders. I might say that when it is not convenient to build an entire new house, the general plan of house herewith described may be used, by fitting up nests inside, making wire runs outside, windows and ventilators, etc. In many places an old chicken-house can be transformed without much trouble or expense into a very good squab-house.

The first and most important fact I wish to impress in regard to buying stock is to buy from a man who **Buying Stock.** makes a business of breeding pigeons. Plenty of such men advertise in the pigeon and poultry papers. It means everything to the beginner to get good birds to start with. Do not buy old birds that have been bred for years with very little vitality and breeding power left in them. They will, of course, disappoint, and no doubt lead you to give up the idea of squab raising with disgust. Good breeders to start with insure success. By good birds I mean strong, healthy, thoroughbred birds, of good size, and from one to three years of age. Do not buy young birds four or five months old, as they will disappoint as much as those that are too old, as it takes them so long to start breeding, and they do not generally raise their first two or three hatchings with much success. Birds from one to one and a half years old are decidedly the best for breeders. A pigeon will breed well until it is eight or ten years old, as a rule. The number of pairs to start with depends entirely on the amount of room that is intended to be given them. If the intending breeder has had no experience with pigeons it would be well to buy ten, or not more than twenty-five pairs to start with. Experience will be gained and additions to the flock may be made as rapidly as your knowledge increases. By keeping your pigeons banded you can keep a record of each bird, which is very advantageous in breeding pigeons for squabs; some squabs breeders claim it is more trouble than it is worth, but I believe in having them banded whenever possible, and have found the record thus kept of untold value to me in the business.

I will not attempt to go into details of description of the various kinds of pigeons, but will only speak of **Best Varieties to Breed.** those breeds we *know* are good for the purpose. I consider the Duchesse the best breed for squab raising, when everything is considered. It is a large bird and the squabs are larger and finer looking than those of the Homer of Dragoon. Of course, some Duchesse pigeons are much larger and finer birds than others for the purpose, but I am speaking of them as a class. They are more domestic than the Homer and are fully as good breeders and feeders, so far as my observation goes, and I have bred a great many of them and have seen others who have done equally as well. Color does not, in my opinion, make much difference with them, but the lightest colored birds should be bred when possible. Some exceptions are taken to the Duchesse on account of its feathered legs; this may be remedied by crossing with the Homer, Runt, or Dragoon. The working Homer, as found almost everywhere, is a splendid breeder and feeder. Fine large birds of this variety can be selected that will give excellent satisfaction. They also do well crossed with the Duchesse or Dragoon. The Dragoon is the next best bird and almost equal to the Homer as to breeding and feeding qualities. It is also a fine show bird and is destined to be one of the most popular show birds in America. Runts are used to advantage by squab breeders, and when crossed with the Homer make large-sized squabs.

The food for breeding birds consists chiefly of good, sound red wheat. Some squab breeders say that they **Food and Feeding.** can use good screenings with as good results as sound wheat. They claim the birds find a variety of different seeds in the screenings that make them appetizing and that the squabs fatten more readily upon them. But my experience differs from this. I cannot believe that it pays as well to buy screenings as it does good wheat, even if the price is more for the latter than the former. There is no waste whatever in feeding good wheat, while there is considerable loss in screenings from the refuse that the birds will not eat. Next in importance to good wheat is good, dry cracked corn. This must not be bought in too large a quantity, owing to its quick absorption of dampness from the air and liability to mould, thereby destroying its value as food for pigeons at once. It should be kept in the driest corner you have and well protected. It should be cracked very coarse, as the finer it is cracked the more loss there is in feeding. A medium-sized grain of corn cracked in two pieces is about the right size. These foods, wheat and corn, are the two staples of food year in and year out. Three feeds of wheat to one of corn should be the proportion for feeding. They should not be fed mixed. Corn may be fed for a week and then wheat for three weeks, or it may be given three feeds of wheat and one of corn. Hemp seed should also always be kept on hand for sick or rundown birds, and once a month give a feed of hemp seed to all, although it is not necessary to do this where hemp seed appears too costly. Canadian peas are excellent food for fattening squabs. No green food is necessary at any time, although lettuce is sometimes given. Stale bread is very

PAIR BLUE RUNTS.

good for a relish occasionally, and the birds will appreciate it very much.

In feeding breeding birds a large part of the food is frequently wasted by giving more at one time than the birds will clean up. Birds feeding their young should be fed twice a day, the first time as soon after daylight as possible, the second time about 3 o'clock in the afternoon, giving the old birds time to fill their young before dark. Just as much feed should be given as the birds will clean up. This can readily be ascertained by measuring the amount in a bucket for a few mornings. If at the second feeding there still remains some of the morning feed reduce the amount until just what is nicely cleaned up is used. Of course, the same number of birds will eat considerably more at one time in the month than another, depending on the number of squabs they are feeding. All this must be looked after closely by the breeder. The best feed-troughs are constructed of twelve-inch boards, from six to twelve feet in length, and putting on sides and ends of three-inch stripping. This will make a low, flat box two inches deep inside. As many troughs may be made as are necessary for the number of birds in the house. One board twelve inches by twelve feet would do for a forty-foot house, although two would be better. In long, low boxes should be plenty of grit at all times; finely ground oyster shells are also very good. A number of different kinds of grit are advertised. A heap of fresh sharp sand should always be near the feeding-troughs. This must be renewed frequently, especially in the Winter season when the birds can not get on the ground outside. Should there be a chance to get some old mortar from a building, or from a heap of mortar left over by masons, it can be used to good advantage the same as sand, and is far better, but it must be pounded up fine and not left in large lumps.

Salt is of the utmost importance to pigeons. A very good way to feed salt is to get it in ten-pound bags, **Salt.** pour sufficient water over it to wet thoroughly and put it in an oven and bake it for a day. It will bake hard, yet still be softer than mineral salt. Should the birds be fed as much soft salt as they would eat, it would kill many, as they would eat too much. I have always used mineral salt in my own houses in large lumps, as it can be bought readily at any store, and I think it will generally give satisfaction; but salt they must have at all times to thrive best. Three or four lumps as big as a cabbage-head in a forty-foot house would be about right. When I say a forty-foot house I mean, also, a house with about six hundred birds. Tobacco stems, to be had at any cigar manu- factory for the hauling away, or at most a trifling cost, should be placed in a pile in one corner of the floor loosely, not too many at one time, but renewed fre- quently, so that the birds may have free access to them for the purpose of building their nests. No other ma- terial ought ever to be used or placed within reach of the birds, as the tobacco aids very largely in keeping away lice, the great pest of the pigeon breeder. Last, but not least, is the water question. Pigeons, to do their best, should have an abundance of pure water for drinking and bathing. Water-boxes, two by four feet and six inches deep, with board covers, are found a very good method to water pigeons. The cover should be movable and contain about five circular holes, five inches in diameter. These covers keep the birds from defiling the water to a large extent, and twice each week the covers should be removed and the birds be permitted to bathe. It is important that birds should have a bath more frequently in warm weather than during Winter; the bath being an effectual way of getting rid of vermin. These boxes should be thoroughly cleaned out each time after the birds bathe, and filled up with fresh water, sufficient boxes being used to supply the wants of the birds. Large tin pans about eighteen inches in diameter and four inches deep, cleaned and filled daily, with no cover, are also used, but having no cover they require more attention. In extremely cold weather hot water should be used sufficient to take the chill off. I believe this will pay for the extra trouble, as Winter is the time above all others that the birds should be doing their best, being the season of high prices.

If your pigeons are already mated, so much the better; if not, select the cocks and hens that you wish to

Breeding and Management.
mate together and put each pair in a box about twelve by twenty-four inches with a separating division in the middle, one bird in each end. Have division made of wire netting so the birds can see each other and "talk the matter over." After keeping them this way for three or four days slip out the division and let the birds together. As a usual thing they will mate up and you will have no further trouble with them. They can then be turned loose in the house. It is always a hard job for the beginner to distinguish the cocks from the hens, but a little practice helps wonderfully in this matter. Cocks as a rule are larger than hens, and in flirting with the hen he will turn around "all the way" frequently, but one rarely sees a hen turn all the way around while cooing and making love to her lord and

master. The best way is to watch them in their attentions to each other, and when you see one bird chasing the other from perch to perch, up and down and all around, you may know that the one doing the chasing is the cock bird, and that likely they are ready to nest. A hen lays but two eggs at a sitting, and usually one day intervenes between the laying of the two eggs. In case you find a nest, however, with four eggs in, you may also find another nest with only one egg in. In that case you would be able to put one of the four in it, providing, of course, that you knew the hen with one egg had laid a sufficient length of time, say three days, to show that she was not going to lay another. In fact, you could easily mark one end with a lead pencil, so that in case another egg was laid you could remove the one you had put in.

Never try to make one hen hatch more than two young, as it will inevitably result in loss. If she does feed them all, at least one, and probably two, will be so poorly fed that they will not amount to anything. Sometimes you will find that where there are only two squabs, one seems to thrive and the other gets along poorly. In such a case take the poorly-fed one to another hen that has only one squab of nearly the same size, and you will find they will both come along all right. If a pair nest and have no eggs, watch the birds carefully and after giving them a fair chance, separate them and give the cock another hen, as the one is no doubt barren, and will do no good as a breeder. Pigeons should be kept in a good, tight house, as warm as it can be made without using artificial heat. Keep the house as clean as possible at all seasons, but especially in hot weather, as the more manure there is in a house the faster the lice seem to breed. If you find that in spite of keeping the house clean and giving the birds plenty of water to bathe in, the lice multiply, something should be done at once to kill them out. I have tried several methods. · The best and surest is to get a small watering-pot with a fine spray, fill it with coal oil and give the perches, empty nests, corners, etc., of breeding-house a liberal dose. It will not hurt the birds and is sure death to the lice. Fine air-slacked lime scattered around is also good. Thousands of young birds are killed every Summer by not keeping the lice under control in houses and lofts. The birds being young do not know so well how to bathe and free themselves of these pests, and they seem to droop from day to day, growing weaker, until finally they die. Coal oil has never killed nor injured a squab or pigeon for me, and I have tried it time and again with best results.

As to diseases I will not say much. If you have a bird that gets down off the perch and droops around, take it out immediately, put it in the ''hospital,'' which should be a small separate loft or large box, where such birds can be kept warm and dry. Then give it plenty of hemp seed, clean water, sand, and a few dry bread crusts. Watch the bird carefully for a week or ten days. If you see no improvement and can not find out the particular cause of the ailment, chop its head off. It is the best cure in such cases. Of course, if one were breeding fancy, high-class pigeons they could nor afford to do this so readily; but a squab breeder, with probably one hundred birds to a fancier's one, cannot afford to devote too much time to any single bird. Some pigeons get a wing disease; the wing droops down and drags on the floor and the bird is hardly able to fly. In such cases pull all the feathers from around the joint. If swollen, paint with tincture of iodine every other day for a week. If not swollen, hold the joint in cold water for say five minutes every day for a week, and keep the bird in a box so that it will not attempt to fly. If it does not then improve, chop its head off. Canker is a bad disease, but not prevalent enough to cause serious uneasiness to a squab breeder. It shows itself by a lump forming in the throat, resembling cheese. It is an inherited disease, and I think as a rule I would kill the old bird that has it, as it is not a good thing to have in your stock.

In dressing squabs for market they should be killed at four weeks old. Some parents will feed their young

Dressing Squabs for Market. better than others and in twenty-five days have them as forward as they would be in twenty-eight days. My rule has always been to go through the house and pick out the ones that seem to be about right, which will generally be just as they first start to leave the nest. After a little practice one can tell almost at a glance whether the squab is sufficiently filled out to kill. What is wanted is large, fat squabs. They should be collected the afternoon of the day before they are to be killed and put in boxes, so that their crops will be emptied of all food at the time of killing. This is important, as the birds look bad and do not keep so well if food is left in their crops after being killed; but the crop can be emptied by squeezing out the grain with the fingers, in case it is not possible to collect all the day before; but this adds much to the work and is entirely unnecessary. I use the common killing-knife, but a good, sharp penknife will answer the purpose. The jugular vein should be cut just back of the head.

The squab should be held for killing in the left hand, the ends of the wings and the legs together in a firm grasp, leaving the head hanging down so that the blood will readily flow out of the cut. Another person should hold the beak of the squab, when convenient, as it is easier that way. Squabs should be picked while warm, as it is much easier done then than after allowing them to get cold, and for this reason the squabs should be killed just as wanted. It seems rather tedious at first to pick a squab, as one has to be careful not to tear the skin, and the pin-feathers are often hard to get out, but after a little practice it will seem much easier. One man who picks from one hundred and fifty to two hundred pairs per week told me that he could pick fourteen squabs clean for market in one hour, but that twelve was his usual number. I never could equal that, but no doubt it could be done. After you have your squab picked clean throw it in ice-cold (or spring) water and leave it in about thirty minutes. This takes out the animal heat and they will keep longer and better. They will also look better as the water seems to plump them out. Now take out the squab and wash off all dirt from feet and blood from around head, fold the wings nicely across the back, tie the two inside legs of a pair together, always putting squabs of about the same size and fatness together, hang up and they are ready to ship.

When ready to ship squabs to market divide them up in the box or boxes so that all the largest and finest

Shipping and Selling. lie together and all the poorest ones by themselves. By so doing you can get better prices, on the average, but you will not have many very poor ones if they are properly looked after. In cold weather it is merely necessary to pack in good, strong boxes, letting a little air in, layer upon layer; pack in boxes holding about six layers, as too many are apt to flatten out of shape and take away that plump, round appearance that goes so far toward getting good prices for them. In Summer put a layer of ice in bottom of box, then put in your squabs, and on top of them, for the last layer, put cracked ice again, then the ice melting and the water trickling down between the birds keeps them nice and cool. In looking for purchasers for squabs you will find if you can give a steady supply week after week, there will be no difficulty in obtaining the best class of customers—private parties, hotels, and fine restaurants. Make the best arrangements you can with them as to prices and numbers they will take for the season, etc. All game stores handle squabs, but the best paying trade is private families, who will take one or two pairs every week the year around and at a fair price. In the markets you can also sell at all times, but not at such good figures. Try to get every private family you can, as you get the best retail price from them. Find out what they have paid and what they will pay. If you live so far from a large city that you can not look up such customers, it would often pay to advertise that families will be supplied, etc., and a good commission house will often obtain very fair prices for you. The best location, however, for a squab raiser is near enough to a large city to be able to get in once a week to look after sales, customers, etc. If you have only a few each week, say one or two dozen pairs, they can easily be put in a canvas case and carried along with you to be delivered as desired.

As to selling price, that depends on the size and condition of squabs and season of the year; from the poorest, thin little things in Mid-summer at twenty cents a pair (that no man who pretends to raise squabs for profit would ever send to market,) to the extra large fat squabs that retail in Mid-winter, all the way up to $1 a pair. Of course, wholesale prices would be from ten to twenty per cent. less than these prices on the same birds. A successful squab raiser ought to be able to retail squabs at an average of sixty cents a pair the year round. This price is for strictly first-class birds; what few second-grade squabs he sells ought to average forty cents a pair the year through, but these last should be very few in number, only from young breeders, etc. With good management a good pair of breeders ought to always clear $1 per year, often more, seldom less. The manure should always figure in the profits at the rate of at least five cents a pair a year. So that if you have five hundred pairs of breeders you could reasonably expect, with good management, to realize a profit of $500 in one year, or $1,000 on one thousand pairs, and in that ratio according to the number of birds you breed. This rate of profit, however, does not include cost of your own labor.

The National Message Holder

FOR HOMING PIGEONS.

THE use of Homing Pigeons as messengers over land and water is gradually increasing in this country, due to the practical application of the wonderful homing instinct of these birds. Their great usefulness for conveying messages has been demonstrated in many ways, especially when no other means of communication are available. The United States Government has messenger pigeon stations at all the principal navy-yards of the Atlantic Coast and at Mare Island, Cal., which are extremely successful. The various coast and trans-atlantic steamship lines use Homing Pigeons to convey messages over the water, and the Chamber of Commerce at San Francisco has established a messenger pigeon service between San Francisco and the Farallone Islands, with a view of utilizing Homing Pigeons for conveying weather reports and shipping news. Many progressive newspapers have established lofts of Homing Pigeons for carrying news and reporting the events of the day. Messenger pigeon service is being utilized to good advantage for professional and business purposes, affording a means of communication that could not be had otherwise. Homing Pigeon fanciers are training their birds for business as well as for fancy purposes, by conveying news from one point to another. These winged messengers are bred by the thousands each year, and their wonderful records of flights are evidences of their worth for fancy and practical purposes.

FIG. 1.
The Holder.

The old way of carrying a message in a quill fastened to the tail-feathers of the bird, has been very unsatisfactory, and is now a thing of the past. Genius has

given a modern method for sending messages safely by Homing Pigeons. The National Message Holder (patented) as shown in Fig. 1, is the best thing that has been invented for this purpose, being the only safe, reliable, and satisfactory method in vogue for sending messages by Homing Pigeons. The National Message Holder is thoroughly covered by patents in the United States and abroad. It is made of aluminum, and weighs only 10 grains, is water-tight, and can be fastened to a bird's leg (see Fig. 2.) in a second instead of minutes as by the old way. It does not impede the flight of the bird and cannot be lost by the dropping of the tail-feathers, as was often the case when the old-style quill was used.

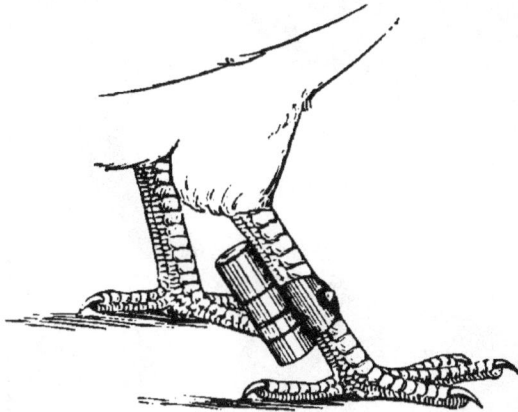

FIG. 2.
Showing Holder Attached to Bird's Leg.

The National Message Holder is used exclusively in the United States Messenger Pigeon Service, being highly endorsed by those in charge of the various stations. Every flyer of pigeons who has used them is loud in praise of their value to the fraternity. To the racing fancier, the National Message Holder will prove a boon, and will save much worry, time and expense of telegrams, by receiving the time of liberation by the bird itself with a certified message from the liberator, which cannot be contested. Again, lost birds can be easily identified as the Holder can be permanently attached to the bird on its record flights, with the owner's name and address, and other instructions written on the blank.

Some Advantages of the National Message Holder.

It is cheap.
It is water-tight.
It does not come off.
It is not noticed by the bird.
It does not irritate the bird.
It can be worn over and over again.
It does not impede the flight of the bird.
It can be worn permanently by the bird.
It affords a sure means of identification.
It saves money, worry, and loss of time.
It can be fastened and unfastened in a second.
It is as light as a feather, weighing only 10 grains.
It is used exclusively by the United States Government.
It is used and endorsed by the most prominent flyers of
  pigeons in the United States and abroad.

TESTIMONIALS.

Please send me one dozen National Message Holders for Homing Pigeons. They are just the thing. Dr. G. H. Stone, Savannah, Ga.

I have used one of your National Message Holders in several instances from business to communicate with my wife at home, attaching the Holder to one of my birds on liberating, and find it a remarkable success.—Geo. G. Hallock, Jr., Brooklyn, N. Y.

The National Message Holder is, without a doubt, the very best means to carry the message. I have considered no other way simply because I believe this Holder superior to any. I leave the Holder attached to the leg long enough so that the bird will not stop to pick at it when you wish the bird to carry a message. Birds that are intended to bring me messages from my patients will have a Holder attached and ready at all times.- Dr. Arnold, Elizabeth, Ills.

A foreign correspondent writes:

"The National Message Holders which you sent me are a great success and answer all the requirements. They do not inconvenience the pigeons in the least, either at rest or on the wing, and the birds hardly notice them when attached to their legs on account of their wonderfully light weight, (only ten grains). The birds do not peck at them, as they used to do with the old goose-quills, to try to work them off. Messages were frequently lost by the birds succeeding in loosening and pulling off the old message quill fastened to the tail-feathers. The new message holder, which is fastened around the leg by means of a clasp, is perfectly secure, and being water-tight, keeps the message intact. Another great advantage is the facility and rapidity with which messages can be sent. With the old goose-quill holder it took from three to five *minutes* to fasten the message on the tail-feathers, with the aluminum holder it takes from three to five *seconds* only, and a large number of pigeons can be forwarded with messages in a very short time by means of this clever device."

PRICES:

Single Holders,......................15 cents each prepaid.
In lots of 10 or more,................12½ cents each prepaid.

We furnish the National Messenger Pigeon Service blanks in books of 50 for 25 cents, books of 100 for 35 cents.

Address all orders and make all remittances payable to

George E. Howard & Co.

504 11th Street N. W.,   Washington, D. C.

THE FEATHER ❧❧

A National Monthly Journal
Devoted to Poultry and Pigeons.

——— PROFUSELY ILLUSTRATED.

The Pigeon Department

The "Pigeon Department" of THE FEATHER has always been appreciated by fanciers of pigeons. The contributors to this department are of the oldest and most competent writers on pigeon topics in this country. Mr. Long, who has it in charge, has been for years a leading judge. He has guided this department since the commencement of THE FEATHER and has done everything to give it the high standing it now has. Some very valuable articles are now being prepared for publication in the "Pigeon Department," and our pigeon readers will enjoy a treat not heretofore had. Many practical articles will be published, and the publishers hope to have each issue a gem in journalism. Unlimited time and expense have been given to the preparation of its articles, and it is believed that better or more practical ones have never been published. THE FEATHER publishes the very best of matter, and its illustrations are numerous and original. It gives its readers the cream of the poultry and pigeon topics of the literary world.

Subscriptions...

Subscriptions may begin at any time. The price of a yearly subscription is 50 cents, but by returning the enclosed coupon to Pigeon Fanciers and 25 cents you get a yearly subscription at half price, besides a copy of THE FEATHER COMPANION AND DIRECTORY. Don't delay sending in your subscription to

GEORGE E. HOWARD & CO.,
504 11th Street N. W.,   **Washington, D. C.**

THE
"Eaton Loft Record"
——OF——
..Homing Pigeon Races

The most complete thing ever gotten up.

EVERY BREEDER AND FLYER OF HOMING PIGEONS...

Should have one or more copies of it. It is endorsed and praised by all who have it, because it tells plainly the record of every mile you have flown.

BY ITS USE YOU CAN TELL AT A GLANCE:

Number of Birds Entered Each Race; Position in Each Race; Returns and Losses; Birds Taken Off; Late Returns; Weather Conditions; and Date and Time of Liberation.

This valuable chart will be sent to any address on receipt of 5 cents, or three copies for 10 cents. Address

GEORGE E. HOWARD & CO.,
504 11th Street N. W.,   **Washington, D. C.**

EMPORIUM of PETS

Headquarters for all kinds of...

Fancy Poultry, Fancy Pigeons, Swans, Pheasants, Canaries, Parrots, Mocking-birds, Cages, Seeds, Gold Fish, Globes, Aquariums, Plants,etc. Monkeys, Dogs, Cats, Squirrels, Rabbits, Guinea Pigs and other Pet Animals.

My specialty is selling first-class Homing Pigeons at $1.00 a pair.

Send for the largest and most complete Illustrated Free Catalogue.

Edw. S. Schmid, 712 12th St. N. W., Washington, D. C.

Sole Agent for
Prairie State Incubators and Brooders for Washington.

Leg Bands For Pigeons and Poultry.. ..

1898 BANDS The official enamelled bands of the Tumbler Clubs are furnished by me at 4 cents each, or 45 cents per dozen, without initials, numbered from 1 up. Aluminum bands for pigeons and poultry, will not tarnish, always the same color; with year and numbered 1 to 100. $3 per 100; with year only, $1.50 per 100; with initials, 25 cents per 100 letters. Send 2-cent stamp for circular and sample. Remittances must accompany order. Enamelled bands, 45 cents per dozen.

T. Willetts, 180 Lawrence St., Lowell, Mass.

∷ The Feather ∷
COMPANION and DIRECTORY
A Handy Reference Book

The demand for this book has been immense. It is handsomely printed and bound in the latest style Persian Golden Brown Waterproof Cover.

This Book Contains:

Calendar for 1898, Calendar of Poultry Keeping, Guide to Practical Poultry Keeping, Glossary of Technical Terms Poultry, The Poultryman's Reference Chart, Standard Breeds of Poultry, The Pigeon Fancier's Chart, Glossary of Technical Terms Pigeons, Standard Varieties of Pigeons, Directory of THE FEATHER Advertisers, Memoranda, Hatching Record, Egg Record, and Show Record Blanks.

What Some Think of It.

AN ENCYCLOPEDIA.

"I find The Companion and Directory an encyclopedia of poultry information."— D. A. MOUNT, proprietor of the Pine Tree Farm, Jamesburg, N. J.

THE BEST BOOK PUBLISHED.

"Feather Companion and Directory is the best book I ever saw on the subject of poultry and will be invaluable to me in breeding same."—JAS. A. DAVIS, Portsmouth, Va.

A REGULAR EDUCATOR.

"We think the Feather Companion and Directory is one of the best and most useful books we have ever seen. It is, in fact, a regular educator; men have come to us and expressed their wonder at how much their birds have improved since they have learned how to treat them by reading the Companion."— A. W. GLUESENKAMP & SON, Batesville, Ind.

A copy of this valuable and instructive book is given FREE to all new subscribers to THE FEATHER, or will be mailed to any address on receipt of 10 CENTS.

GEORGE E. HOWARD & CO., Publishers,
Washington, D. C.

93

Poultry Supplies 🌹 🌹 🌹

New York and Export Agents for

Prairie State Incubators and Brooders.

—o—
We carry a full line of

**Mann's, Wilson's, Chapman's, Webster & Hannum's,
Dandy, Standard, and Premier**

Green Bone and Vegetable Cutters,

PRICE $5.00 to $350.00 EACH.

according to style and size of machine.

NOTICE.—AS AN EGG PRODUCER OUR...

BANNER EGG FOOD AND TONIC

CAN NOT BE EQUALLED.

It does exactly whatever we say it will do, as thousands of Poultrymen can tell you.

Price, 1-lb. can 25c., five 1-lb. cans $1.00; one Case of two dozen 1-lb. cans $1.00.

**Agents..
Wanted.**

**Discounts
to the
Trade.**

CHICK MANNA.

If you feed it to your young chickens, you can raise 90 per cent. of your production up to maturity.

Price, 10c. per lb.; 5-lb package 40c.; 15-lb. package $1.10.

—o—

NOTICE.—We are the sole Agents for New York City and vicinity for

LAMBERT'S DEATH TO LICE.

POWDER AND OINTMENTS.

Large stock always on hand for immediate shipment.

—o—

OUR IMMENSE

ILLUSTRATED CATALOGUE FREE.

It tells you what you want in the line of General Supplies and for successful Poultry Raising.

CORRESPONDENCE SOLICITED.

Address

Excelsior Wire & Poultry Supply Co.

28 Vesey St., NEW YORK CITY.

Wm. V. RUSS, Prop.

www.ingramcontent.com/pod-product-compliance
Lightning Source LLC
Chambersburg PA
CBHW031445270326
41930CB00007B/870